NETWORK MARKETING:

The Real Strategy That Converts
People into Customers

© Copyright 2018 by Carmine Rea - All rights reserved.

The following eBook is reproduced below with the goal of providing information that is as accurate and reliable as possible. Regardless, purchasing this e-book can be seen as consent to the fact that both the publisher and the author of this book are in no way experts on the topics discussed within and that any recommendations or suggestions that are made herein are for entertainment purposes only. Professionals should be consulted as needed prior to undertaking any of the action endorsed herein.

This declaration is deemed fair and valid by both the American Bar Association and the Committee of Publishers Association and is legally binding throughout the United States.

Furthermore, the transmission, duplication, or reproduction of any of the following work including specific information will be considered an illegal act irrespective of if it is done electronically or in print. This extends to creating a secondary or tertiary copy of the work or a recorded copy and is only allowed with an express written consent from the Publisher. All additional rights reserved.

The information in the following pages is broadly considered a truthful and accurate account of facts. As such, any inattention, use, or misuse of the information in question by the reader will render any resulting actions solely under their purview. There are no scenarios in which the publisher or the original author of this work can be in any fashion deemed liable for any hardship or damages that may befall them after undertaking information described herein.

Additionally, the information in the following pages is intended only for informational purposes and should thus be thought of as universal. As befitting its nature, it is presented without assurance regarding its prolonged validity or interim quality. Trademarks that are mentioned are done without written consent and can in no way be considered an endorsement from the trademark holder.

TABLE OF CONTENTS

Introduction 1

CHAPTER 1:
How to Protect Yourself in Network Marketing & the Changes within Marketing Practices from Traditional to Digital 3

CHAPTER 2:
How to Use YouTube to Find Larger Audience and Build Trust with Viewers 8

CHAPTER 3:
Combine YouTube with Facebook for an Even Bigger Impact 12

CHAPTER 4:
How a Website Will Help Your Business – A Guide for Creating a Website or Professional Landing Page so That Potential Buyers Have a Specific Location to View and Purchase Products 16

CHAPTER 5:
Use Facebook Ads to Direct Traffic to Your Website – Why Facebook Ads Are a Smart Investment to Help Build Awareness about Your Product 21

CHAPTER 6:
Using Video Presentations to Tell a Story – Steps to Use Expressive and Informative Video to Offer Value to Potential Customers 27

CHAPTER 7:

Facebook Groups for Your Business & in the Beginning, Don't Base Success on Money 30

Conclusion 34

INTRODUCTION

Converting people into customers has never been equally as challenging and rewarding as our current digital age. Given the myriad of changes that the digital age has brought forth, including rapid changes to the manner with which consumers shop for their products, to the breadth of information available online on an abundance of topics, the online marketplace has now shifted away from traditional practices to a modern online arena.

Evidently, Network Marketing is more than just another marketing strategy to boost revenue. This approach is crucial to building relationships and trust amongst your customers so that your business can grow and maximize its exposure to target audiences online and in other areas. Even more, you have the obligation to utilize all of the various strategies to reach your target audience and spread the message of your brand. These strategies include creating a YouTube channel and initiating a Facebook Ads campaign. Thereafter, combining these two approaches will further enhance your appeal to audiences through a multi-pronged approach.

Leveraging these methods of marketing, coupled with creating a professional landing page, and website for your business will allow you to access a coveted customer base and become a viable player in the digital marketplace. Learning how to implement these online marketing strategies is paramount for your ability to navigate the digital market and have a pulse on upcoming digital trends.

Once you are equipped with these business-altering marketing approaches, your company will emerge from the plethora of competitors and soar above the marketplace on a continual basis.

CHAPTER 1

HOW TO PROTECT YOURSELF IN NETWORK MARKETING & THE CHANGES WITHIN MARKETING PRACTICES FROM TRADITIONAL TO DIGITAL

Now that traditional brick and mortar stores are consistently becoming less relevant, your ability to utilize the online marketplace is incredibly important to convert people into lifelong customers of your business. Moreover, as audiences migrate online, it is paramount that your business' marketing strategies are able to adjust to these shifting trends. If not, your business will likely fail to reach targeted revenue marks and you may be forced to overspend on additional marketing campaigns to compensate.

Network marketing employs a range of marketing strategies that reach audiences and boosts audience awareness of your business. Specifically, network marketing depends on a broad range of distributors for maximum growth. This direct-selling method of marketing is reliant on select independent agents to create a distribution network for services and products. In a digital age, however, this arena is significantly altered due to the pervasive nature of the internet. In other words, as customers for your product and or service are increasingly going online to shop and search for specific items, goods, and services, your business marketing model must adapt to these changing audience trends in order to earn revenue for your business.

As a business, acclimating to the expansive nature of cyberspace especially when trying to reach niche audiences, striving to turn them into viable and loyal customers is a necessity. Furthermore, adapting to the many shifting consumer trends is even more important because of the pace at which the internet is continually changing. Indeed, cyberspace has now become the new marketplace for consumers who are further used to immediate gratification for their shopping and overall acquisition of products and services from a range of businesses. As an advertiser, marketer, and businessman, your ability to adapt and anticipate audience trends online are incredibly important for your success in turning regular people into customers for your business.

So, what exactly is marketing? Marketing is the systematic process and planning of an organization's overall promotional efforts and campaigns. Moreover, this is truly a larger umbrella term that includes various forms of public relations and advertising methods.

Nevertheless, marketing is focused on the promotion of services and products with the marked intention of driving sales. The audiences for marketing, as opposed to public relations, are primarily potential buyers and customers. Also, the interaction of marketers with the media is entirely through the form of paid media. This means that marketers work from a given budget to develop and implement marketing campaigns, rather than "pitching" journalists and media members for organic coverage of their products and or services.

In a digital age, marketing encompasses methods and factors that marketers of previous eras never had to consider. Among these, for instance, is the need to create content that is "social-by-design." This idea refers to the notion that marketing content must entice online users to want to share on their social media profiles. In doing so, your marketing content can maximize its exposure as it will not only reach your targeted audience but will proliferate across their entire social media profile with hundreds, maybe thousands of other users online. In this way, your business can reach a plethora of potential customers simply by producing content that can be shared online. In addition, creating content that entices users to share on their own profiles and engage with your marketing is a great way to boost your favorability among users online. In the process, your business will be seen as trendy and in touch with relevant cultural phenomena, rather than stale and unable to adapt to shifting changes within the cultural sphere.

In the current digitally-driven arena of network marketing, producing content that speaks to audiences in a relevant, engaging, and creative manner is critical for converting people into customers of your business. Traditionally, marketing strategies utilized tabloids, pamphlets, flyers, newspapers, billboards, magazine placements, and other forms of traditional media to boost audience awareness and gain exposure. While some of these approaches may still be relevant, albeit, in a severely limited context, digital marketing is of primary importance in the modern age. In fact, if traditional methods are to be used, they should be as an appendage to complement existing digital marketing campaigns that are already in place for a particular product or service. Indeed, this is the best way to reach target audiences and ensure that you are creating customers from the online users that you reach through your marketing.

In the current digital age, the legal frameworks that govern the internet are becoming increasingly insufficient and outdated. With the expansive nature of the internet, the abundance of legal implications pertaining to cyberspace is not surprising. However, the fluidity and decentralized nature of the online environment starkly contrasts the rigid and concrete disposition of legal frameworks. Not to mention, sole dependence on laws for internet regulation requires leaning on national legal frameworks for a transnational medium. In my opinion, persisting with this approach will contribute to the existing disparity with regards to access on information, better known as the Digital Divide, as certain regional laws inhibit access to platforms available in other areas of the world. Since the rise of new media allows for the mass dissemination of ideas through various technological methods of delivery, copyright and intellectual property laws are more important than ever before. Devoid of the capacity to acquire and maintain reasonable compensation for their work, current producers may feel forced to forfeit their creative endeavors due to an inability to afford further production. Additionally, the lack of intellectual property protection could dissuade promising future content and information producers from contributing to the creative economy altogether.

As a business applying marketing strategies online, you are well advised to acquire sound legal counsel that is experienced with the intricate and complex legal issues of cyberspace. In this way, you will ensure that your network marketing practices online are protected against possible litigation. Also, acquiring legal counsel through copyright protection for these online marketing practices will protect your original content from being stolen and or redistributed by imposters or competitors.

Protecting yourself through legal measures online is an important way to ensure that your efforts and budgeting for digital marketing do not go to waste. Employing practical protective measures, in this way, is crucial for your business.

CHAPTER 2

HOW TO USE YOUTUBE TO FIND LARGER AUDIENCE AND BUILD TRUST WITH VIEWERS

As YouTube is a visual medium, it is highly recommended that you utilize YouTube to its full advantage when developing and implementing your digital marketing approach.

Buying ad space on YouTube's platform, such as 15 or 30-second commercial spots, is a beneficial method of boosting your online profile and target niche audiences in the digital age. The average cost of buying a YouTube ad spot is rated on a per-view basis. Advertisers will pay-per-view of each ad which can range from $0.10 to $0.30. An added benefit with YouTube's advertising platform is that each view of your ad counts toward your total YouTube views. As a result, you can simultaneously increase the total views for your YouTube channel by buying ad space and reaching a large audience. Similar to the other social media outlets, YouTube allows you to target a specific age, locations, and genders. Overall, marketers have to pay more, on a rolling incremental basis, for targeting specific niche audiences through their digital marketing strategies.

YouTube's overall global audience is only continuing to grow. As more and more businesses are developing content that is user-friendly with videos, YouTube is a coveted platform for marketers and advertisers that are seeking to reach their target audience in the digital arena. What's more, millennial is the primary demographic that uses YouTube. If you are planning on targeting a younger audience for your products and or services, YouTube is a great vehicle through which this younger audience base can be reached. Even more, through using YouTube, your cache and reputation with audiences will become stronger as you will be equated with a trendy social media platform. As a result, this will grow your level of trust with viewers, thereby boosting your ability to convert viewers into loyal customers of your business and earn more revenue.

The best way to start using YouTube to find a larger audience is to create a YouTube page for your business. This page is incredibly useful for allowing you to create your own content without having to outsource marketing costs to a third party firm or broaden your budget to a significant extent. Moreover, this page also gives you the option of telling your brand's story through a very popular visual medium that connects to younger audiences, in particular. Remember, the goal of content creation is to create content that separates itself from the competition. With YouTube, and specifically, a YouTube channel for your business, you can speak to your target audience on a more consistent basis through a relevant medium.

At an affordable rate, YouTube advertising is an excellent way to boost your online presence and find a larger audience for your business. For businesses especially, viewers directly engage with your marketing content because it is not a rudimentary advertisement and can also be very entertaining depending on whether you are able to inject creativity into your content. Indeed, this overall enhancement of views from an audience can add credibility to your business. Incidentally, this can lead to increased exposure for your business while also building a unique relationship with your target audience. Not to mention, the added views on YouTube will also increase your overall impression online. This is to say, with more views on YouTube from both your target audience as well as new audience members that your marketing content has attracted, your business will appear in an increased amount of organic searches both on YouTube and online search engines that are used by nearly all active cyberspace users (Google, in particular).

When creating marketing content for your business on YouTube, there is no need to try and produce a "viral" video. Rather, you are best served to create content that speaks to your target audience in a creative, compelling, and informative manner that speaks to your brand's best qualities while also conveying the notion that your business is intriguing. The same can be said for the manner with which your content presents the specific products and or services of your business.

Cultivating a YouTube channel for your brand and or business is an extremely effective way of broadening your audience and telling the "story" of your business. This avenue of marketing also gives you the opportunity to continually educate your audience and customer based on topics pertaining to your business. Keep in mind that consistency is the key and the best content is consistent content especially when it relates to your business and the products and or services that it offers.

A helpful tip concerning creating marketing content on YouTube (or any other online platform, for that matter), is to refrain from producing anything that is too controversial. This includes posts that are too political or openly endorse a particular candidate, polarizing social issues, etc. If certain issues divide the general public, there is a good chance that your target audience and potential customer base will be divided by those issues as well. Therefore, remember to remain committed to producing content that is inclusive and relevant to your business, along with its products and or services and your brand's story.

In this digital age, it is incumbent for you to create content that allows audiences to feel gratified. In this age, audiences are accustomed to instant gratification in all aspects of their lives, especially with regards to the content that they consume and engage with on a regular basis. This is precisely why visual content through YouTube videos is very beneficial for your business as this avenue of content delivery and marketing allows you to cater to your audiences' demands and take full advantage of recent consumer trends in today's marketplace.

CHAPTER 3

COMBINE YOUTUBE WITH FACEBOOK FOR AN EVEN BIGGER IMPACT

That's right, combining two extremely popular and useful online platforms for your marketing strategy is a great way to boost your appeal with audiences, as well as expanding your potential customer base. Building business connections by combining both of the platforms will elevate your appeal to audiences so that your business can target a broader potential customer base, as well as appeal to your "base" of customers which are already in place and loyal to your business.

Here are 4 steps for combining your YouTube channel with your Facebook page:

1) Navigate your browser to the upload page on YouTube.
2) Then, scroll to the page's section labeled "Activity Sharing." This section will have certain buttons that will allow you to link your YouTube channel with other social media platforms of yours, including Twitter and Facebook.
3) Click on the Facebook link to open a brand new Facebook window in your browser. Thereafter, this new window will then prompt you to log in so that you can use your Facebook account with your YouTube channel.

4) Now, enter the email address for your Facebook account followed by the password, followed by clicking "Log in." The Facebook window will then close and YouTube's "Sharing Activity" section will now say that your YouTube and Facebook account is now linked together.

Alas! Your online marketing strategy now enjoys a symbiotic relationship that conjoins two of the most popular and effective online platforms to reach audiences and promote your business' products and services. After connecting both your YouTube channel and Facebook accounts, be sure to keep in mind that because your content is now linked through all of your online platforms, all of your marketing content is available to *both* audiences. This is to say, your YouTube audience and Facebook audience have access to the same content. This certainly carries the benefit of targeting both audiences at once, but also requires that you remain mindful that the content you create is transferable to both YouTube and Facebook. In other words, if you create written advertisements for your business, this content will not be transferable to YouTube. Therefore, be sure to confine written content to *only* your Facebook account. Granted, your video content can be shared on both YouTube and Facebook now that the two accounts have been linked with each other for maximum exposure and effectiveness in reaching your target audience.

Combining both your YouTube and Facebook accounts will help you boost your YouTube views, in particular. Because Facebook is still the leading social media site, featuring your YouTube content on Facebook will undoubtedly attract many of your Facebook followers to your

YouTube channel. Indeed, this will add subscribers to your YouTube channel which is particularly helpful when you are in the early stages of establishing your business' YouTube page. In fact, in 2016 study, researchers found that, of the top viral YouTube videos, a significant percentage of the views were from audiences on Facebook. This is significant because it highlights the value of linking your YouTube channel with your Facebook page for added views, subscribers, and overall engagement with your online marketing content.

Employing online marketing strategies that "step outside of the box," so to speak, is paramount to your success as an online marketer. What's more, your business will gain significant exposure from these strategic approaches while also emerging from the shadow of competitors so that you can dominate your market and convert people into customers of your business. Moreover, Facebook gives precedent to those posts with videos that are uploaded directly to Facebook's platform. However, YouTube videos have secondary importance and can still serve to enhance your exposure to target audiences for your business. This is encouraging because it highlights how your business' original Facebook marketing content can remain a priority on the platform, even when combining your account with your YouTube channel. In this way, your marketing content, whether it be on YouTube or Facebook, will never go to waste. As a result, you do not have to worry about overspending or wasting away your business' marketing budget.

One of the added benefits of creating a YouTube channel and linking it to your Facebook account is that this process is free. While

Facebook Ads requires a budget and competing in an advertising auction, developing a YouTube channel is free and can save you a lot of money on your marketing budget. Granted, advertising on YouTube also requires a budget, creating a channel and producing content from that channel your audience is free and very effective.

The more Facebook users engage with your YouTube video, the more popularity, and visibility it receives from Facebook. Facebook will increase the viewability of your YouTube video post if the interaction increases with each post. This is encouraging for you as it reveals that the more videos you promote, the better viewability and promotion it will receive from Facebook.

CHAPTER 4

HOW A WEBSITE WILL HELP YOUR BUSINESS – A GUIDE FOR CREATING A WEBSITE OR PROFESSIONAL LANDING PAGE SO THAT POTENTIAL BUYERS HAVE A SPECIFIC LOCATION TO VIEW AND PURCHASE PRODUCTS

Having an online page outside of Facebook and YouTube is an important "home base" for your business that can provide valuable information to your current and future customers. Even more, having a website for your business also gives you the option of plugging your other social media sites right on your website. For instance, a webpage for your business could allow you to post your YouTube and Facebook links, and maybe even share some of your content form those platforms directly onto your webpage as well. A landing page of this manner will give you a multi-pronged approach to your growing online marketing strategy.

More importantly, though, a webpage or professional landing page is a great arena for your business to sell its products and promote its services. Think of your webpage as an informative "launchpad" for your business, or as a "cyber-pamphlet" that gives your customers a way to purchase your products, and or learn more about what your business offers.

An excellent online resource for developing a webpage for your businesses is Squarespace. This application is very easy to use and can be applied by anyone with a rudimentary understanding and ability for computers and technology. A helpful tip for establishing a website is identifying how attuned to navigating the internet your customer base is. While this may seem like a silly and unnecessary question to ask, especially if your business has been running for a long time, however, you must consider the likelihood of your customers preferring to learn about your products in-store or through traditional mediums such as pamphlets. Granted, this is likely only applicable to businesses that have a much older customer base.

Another worthwhile tip for creating a website is making sure that the syntax and layout of the webpage are clear and concise. A major mistake that many businesses make when creating a website is overloading their page with information and a "busy" layout that can cause confusion amongst viewers of your page. Instead, structure the layout of your page with compelling images of your products and with engaging color schemes. Coupled with this layout, your syntax should include only the most pertinent information that describes your business in the most effective manner, rather than elaborating on every single aspect of your business. This gives your audience awareness for the most important information about your business and its products. With this added clarity, you elevate the professional appeal of your business. In doing so, your customers will be more trusting of buying products from your webpage, without the apprehension and worry of having their personal financial information compromised online.

Developing trust with your customers is the key to growing your business, especially online. In an era of distrust in many of our societal institutions, notably the media and government, businesses have an obligation to foster trust in consumers. Moreover, this trust begins with the products and services that businesses offer their customers. When consumers can trust your business with their money every time they are making purchases in the online marketplace, your online platforms, be it social media or your business' webpage, will continue to grow and polish their appeal to audiences.

Here are 4 helpful tips for creating an effective professional webpage for your business:

1) Plan the website in advance and decide which content you will include and not include on its pages.
2) Outsource the management of the webpage, or assign employees to specifically manage the page for your business.
3) Put together a plan for how the information and structure of the webpage will flow throughout the various pages of the site.
4) Be sure to develop the user interface so that you are aware of the experience that your customers and potential customers have when visiting your webpage.

These outlined tips will help your site develop in a systematic fashion with consideration of clarity and concision in mind. Before you start your website, you are required to register your domain name online. This can be done by registering the domain name through an ISP or even through a registration company that specializes in domain names. Choosing a domain name that captures your business is very important in the case of your business' names being unavailable for a domain name.

To enhance your online presence, you first need to ensure that your webpage actually works effectively. For obvious reasons, this is the most important aspect of your webpage. Consistency is the key! An active online presence that is consistent both in presentation and connectivity is paramount to having a successful and effective webpage for your business.

When planning for your webpage, there are some very important questions that you must ask to clarify your direction and presentation. Here are questions that you need to consider:

- Who is your target audience?
- What information will your audience expect?
- What do your competitors offer on their websites?
- How will your website support your overall business strategy?
- What business processes can you incorporate into the functionality of your website?
- Will the website be developed internally or be outsourced?
- What is your budget for the website's initial development? What about ongoing maintenance?

Strive to tailor the content and services on your webpage so that it specifically matches your audience's level of knowledge. Moreover, a website intended mostly for subject experts and repeat visitors should be formulated differently than a website tailored to the general public.

If, for instance, your audience is knowledgeable about your business, its services and subject matter, introductory information can then be buried deeper into the website and the user interface can thereby be streamlined for faster loading on the webpage itself. In the same way, frequent users of your website generally know where they want to go. Therefore, your website should allow users to navigate quickly to reach and engage with specific content or services.

Supporting and supplementing your business strategy with your website is an excellent way to ensure that you are maximizing the full potential of your business. Specifically, you should clearly state what business goal(s) you are aiming to support with your website online. Moreover, a business website that aims to reduce and limit shipping expenses through providing official documents online will have a particularly different design, structure, and layout than a website that strives to increase product sales online. Furthermore, if your business website is effectively managed and designed, it will automate your common business processes as well as helping to increase its productivity. Customer service calls, especially, can be mostly reduced so long as your website performs the following services to your customers:

- Allows your customers the option to pay, order for your products, and services.
- Provides project status as well as shipping information.
- Provides each of your customers with specific information and documents pertaining to the products and or services of your business.

CHAPTER 5

USE FACEBOOK ADS TO DIRECT TRAFFIC TO YOUR WEBSITE – WHY FACEBOOK ADS ARE A SMART INVESTMENT TO HELP BUILD AWARENESS ABOUT YOUR PRODUCT

Facebook's broad user base is very helpful for advertising online as it provides a platform that gives you many options. Here, businesses are able to choose from an abundant range of multiple advertising options, which include, but aren't limited to, different display advertisements and sprawling newsfeeds on users' screens. Indeed, your customers will likely be the one most familiar with Facebook Ads given the simple fact that most of them likely use Facebook on a regular to semi-regular basis.

Facebook's lead ads platform gives you options for linking users to an alternate page that offers way more information pertaining to a certain product that they are interested in. In addition, other advertising forms that are available on Facebook are advertising carousels, Canvas ads, and search ads. In the coming months, Facebook will be introducing Facebook Messenger advertising to further broaden your ability to reach users on Facebook's coveted platform.

With the proliferation of a multitude of social media platforms, Facebook continues to lead the social media category in content sharing, user-usage rates, and corporate advertising, and marketing. However, this usage is not confined to older demographics or just those users and potential customers with specific niche interests, but rather a wide range of users from a plethora of demographics, geographic regions, devices, and financial and equational backgrounds. With such a broad audience, there is little surprise that Facebook Ads garners a lot of revenue for the platform from various companies and entrepreneurs such as you, who are seeking ways to broaden their reach, boost awareness for their products and services, and convert users into customers.

Creating and Ads with Facebook is incredibly beneficial for your business because it allows you to tap into the online social media behavior of your customers, thereby augmenting your online marketing approach. Moreover, Canvas ads give users an option to click on a particular ad and view a full-screen advertisement that has videos, images, and myriad other features that are both engaging and interactive. Upon finishing the viewing of the ad, users can then return to Facebook without the hassle of having to reopen and or close certain screens that were already available. Companies that have employed Canvas advertising have reported extremely significant increases in lead quality, as well as a significant reduction in the overall cost of lead advertising. Given that Facebook is a premier company that prides itself on its own consistently refining platform, you are guaranteed continual improvement to your marketing strategy simply by virtue of the fact that Facebook is always looking for new methods of improvement.

Facebook advertising offers your business increasingly expanding options to reach your target audience and convert them into customers. What's more, the cost of this approach is affordable and will not cause strain to your budget. Making use of the many options available for growing your business, in this way, will ensure that your business maximizes its potential for gaining revenue and earnings sizeable profit. Not to mention, you should utilize Facebook, for instance, to gain the most exposure for your business and develop a relationship with your audience.

Building awareness for your product and business as a whole should be a major priority for your strategy. Using Facebook, for instance, is one of the most effective ways to build this awareness simply because of the sheer number of people who use Facebook. What's more, user engagements on Facebook also include users sharing articles, advertisements and yes, even the profile page for your business. Making use of user behavior on Facebook will undoubtedly boost exposure for our business and the products and or services that your business provides.

Measuring user engagement in this fashion gives you a marketplace edge as it will allow you to predict and adapt to user trends, along with the changing trends within your specific target audience. Furthermore, the accuracy of Facebook's advertising options allows your ads to be used in the most effective manner, thereby avoiding wasted budgetary funds, effort, and time. Keep in mind that Facebook is a very business-friendly platform, offering relatively affordable ad rates that are exceptionally accurate in reaching your target audience, be it domestically and or globally. With the abundance of publishers on Facebook, advertising on this platform allows you to gain exposure with audiences outside of Facebook as well. Moreover, when striving to drive traffic to your website through Facebook Ads, you will need to consider forms of advertisements that will entice users to engage with and share.

Given how powerful and pervasive Facebook is for advertising (among other uses), there are still myriad companies that aren't using Facebook's platform. For those that are, however, they are doing so without an effective and well-planned strategic approach. Using Facebook and, more importantly, using Facebook with a creative advertising strategy will elevate your position to earn audience attention and marketplace positioning that you may have otherwise missed out on attaining.

In order to figure out which advertisements are most relevant to certain users on its platform, Facebook often uses an online auction model on its site designed to maximize the overall advertising and marketing experiences for businesses and users. First, the auction starts with an advertiser submitting a request for their advertisement to be shown to users within its targeted range. To submit their request, advertisers are required by Facebook to define what their target niche audience is before engaging in the auction that the site puts together, set a campaign objective, and then place a particular value that they desire from the final outcome of their advertisement, like conversions and clicks, for example. The monetary value placed by advertisers is formally called a "bid" on Facebook. Then, whenever there exists an opportunity to show a certain ad to a user in the advertiser's previously defined target audience, an auction is then held to determine whether the users will see that particular advertisement or a different ad altogether. In this way, Facebook runs billions of auctions every day so that users are paired with only the most relevant advertisements for their respective Facebook feeds.

Facebook's advertising platform also allows you to use geotargeting and specific device targeting to reach your target audience and maximize awareness for your business and product. Employing these measures for your Facebook marketing strategy are innovative ways to elevate your online marketing approach while also expanding your reach using Facebook Ads. For an official definition, geotargeting is an online marketing practice that uses personalized online content based on the specific geographic locations of potential buyers. So, if a user is living in Toronto and opens a webpage, they will be viewing advertising content tailored to their specific location. Moreover, this content could include events related to your particular area like music and or film festivals that will attract niche audiences.

Geotargeting can play a crucial role in developing marketing strategies that are aligned with reaching niche audiences online. Businesses that employ geotargeting on Facebook Ads will gain remarkable benefits and will broaden their online exposure and reach. Not to mention, industry studies have shown that businesses that use geotargeting within their marketing strategy tend to gain more audience awareness for their products and or services than competitors who refrain from employing such practices.

As Facebook's users are checking their newsfeed and profiles consistently throughout the day, your advertising content has many opportunities to be exposed to the preferred target audience in your marketing strategy.

CHAPTER 6

USING VIDEO PRESENTATIONS TO TELL A STORY – STEPS TO USE EXPRESSIVE AND INFORMATIVE VIDEO TO OFFER VALUE TO POTENTIAL CUSTOMERS

Video presentations are an important way to express your business' values, commitments, and aspects of your products and services. There are numerous strategies for effective video presentations that add value to potential customers. Furthermore, to convert customers into potential customers, communicating effectively is crucial. Indeed, as mentioned earlier in the YouTube video chapter, videos are great vehicles for maximizing exposure and telling the story of your business, brand, products, and services. With the increasing demand for instant gratification, video content for online marketing will boost the appeal of your business.

Notably, effective video presentations have key attributes of communication. Whether the video is content heavy, with a voice-over reading the content on the screen, or if there is a speaker in front view that is speaking to the camera, your video presentation should be expressive, engaging, and informative for viewers. There is no doubt that great video presentations dovetail with effective communication skills and practices.

The process of video presentations for you can be very daunting. Nevertheless, this approach is incredibly worthwhile to offer value to potential customers. This is due to the fact that our brains are able to process visual information 60,000 times faster than just words, and one minute of video content can be considered equivalent to nearly 1.9 million words. Also, video presentations are useful because of business. This is to say that content-based and particularly video-based marketing are said to enhance marketing leads by 510% and revenue by more than 5x!

Keep in mind when producing video content for your online business marketing that the overall goal of any video is not to sell a certain product or service, but rather to provide a combination of information and entertainment.

Here are a few tips for producing video content for your business:

1) **Don't Be Cheap**. Investing in great, high-quality equipment is the key to your success in creating entertaining and informative video content. While you certainly do not need to spend 25k on a camera or video-edging equipment, making a viable investment in good equipment will elevate your content and ensure that it appears credible, professional, and engaging.

    The quality of your video content will determine the quality of your customers. So, make sure that your videos are presented in a manner that will attract the highest quality customer for your business.

2) **Practice, Practice, Practice!** It's true, the more you practice anything, the better you will be at it. The same is true for

producing video content and familiarizing yourself with the technology necessary for creating great video content. Because filming and editing practice requires skill, you should familiarize yourself as much as possible so that your content, once finally produced, will stand out from the competition and attain the results you seek.

When appearing on camera, be sure to wear colors that appear well on camera. Typically, darker colors are preferred as opposed to bright colors. Also, try to speak in a "natural" tenor. Whether you are trying to appear too perfect or not, being natural is far more effective in presenting your business and its products in a positive and, more importantly, a relatable manner.

3) **Speak Your Brand.** Anytime you are speaking publicly about your business and or its products, having a good idea of your brand in your presentation is very important. This is important because knowing your brand will give your presentation a clearer tone and message, while also giving credibility to your business as a polished and professional company.

Remember, if you are not clear on your brand, message, and tone, how can you expect your audience and potential customers to be?

CHAPTER 7

FACEBOOK GROUPS FOR YOUR BUSINESS & IN THE BEGINNING, DON'T BASE SUCCESS ON MONEY

Whether to create a Facebook group for your business or not is a decision that will not carry great consequence for your overall online marketing strategy. Rather, this decision pertains to whether you decide to limit the number of users that are allowed to gain access to your business' Facebook page. You are well advised to keep your Facebook page open to all users instead of closing the group and requiring each new user to be "permitted" to join the group.

Frankly, forcing members to request permission to join your Facebook group is a dangerous and very ineffective online strategy. What's more, this approach could turn users away from wanting to join your page and learn more about your business. Also, any online marketing strategy that you employ should operate under the policy of being open to all current and potential customers. Having a closed group option for your business' Facebook page only closes your business off from increasing exposure among coveted potential customers. Not to mention, if certain customers are closed off from learning more about your business online, they are more likely to gravitate to your competitors.

In an age of instant gratification in this digital era, you should not bar your audience form accessing information concerning your business. This not only goes against current digital consumer trends but also gives leverage to your competitors. Remember to use Facebook to its full advantage; that is, accessing its breadth of users for maximum exposure for your business.

The sole benefit of having a closed Facebook group for your business is that it could give your current customers a feeling of inclusiveness and appreciation. Not to mention, this closed group could also give you the option of offering exclusive deals and promotions to your customer base that they would otherwise not have access to. In this way, you may consider this approach for your current customers. However, for attracting new customers, your Facebook page should remain open and accessible for every potential customer.

When starting your online network marketing strategy, remember that your success should not be based solely on the revenue that you generate. Instead, a lasting direct sales company should first be built on the *relationships* you build and trust you establish with your clients. Indeed, building and sustaining trust and worthwhile relationships is fundamental to building a thriving business, especially one that utilizes network marketing strategies in the digital age.

Creating a lasting direct sales company depends upon the key ideas of trust, relationships, sustainability, and ethical practice. Devoid of these examples, your direct sales company in the modern digital age will suffer greatly. Another important idea to consider for your business when trying to build trust with potential customers is the notion that consumers have limited loyalty, generally. This is to say, once you make critical mistakes, like confusing an online order or compromising valuable financial information, your customers will likely flock to competitors that are more buttoned-up in these areas. So, ensuring that your business practice is ethical and trustworthy will certainly go a long way in helping you establish a lasting and sustainable direct sales company for years to come.

Extremely successful companies like Avon, Amway, Herbalife, and Nu Skin have implemented these strategies to their fullest potential and are certainly reaping the tremendous benefits. These benefits are not confined to mere revenue and financial gain; however, they also include customer loyalty and sustainability. As a result, these companies can continue to target their loyal customer bases while also pursuing new potential customers that will only further boost their already established, trusted, and well-known brand names.

When these brands were first starting, they created their brands by establishing trust with their customers and then shifting their focus on acquiring more revenue. If, for example, the focus in direct marketing strategy is on revenue, then your business is at a great disadvantage due to failing to build a solid reputation with customers. These industry-specific examples are very important and valuable as you proceed in developing a marketing strategy for direct sales.

While a great idea for your product and or service is the key, establishing trust like many successful direct sales companies have done in the past, is incredibly important as well, especially considering the notion that direct sales involve face-to-face interactions. If a customer respects and trusts your company and brand, they are more likely to return as customers in the future and recommend your products to their friends, family, and acquaintances.

CONCLUSION

Thank you for making it through to the end of *Network Marketing: The Real Strategy That Converts People into Customers*, let's hope it was informative and able to provide you with all of the tools you need to achieve your goals, whatever they may be.

The next step is to begin implementing the strategies presented in your current online marketing strategy. Or, you can selectively merge these tactics into the strategies you are already employing for your business. Note that each business operates individually and not every strategy is directly applicable at exactly the same time for every single business venture. Nonetheless, you will find that this e-book provides comprehensive methods of maximizing online exposure through merging a few key forms of online marketing such as YouTube videos with your Facebook page.

Do not forget the importance of video content! In the modern digital age, more than any age prior, video content captures audience attention more effectively than ever before. As a result, your customers will appreciate your branding message while also gaining valuable and readily available information pertaining to your business. Now, these details certainly require sharpening your communication skills, luckily this e-book provides you with critical keys for successful oral communication and presentation!

A crucial component of your network marketing strategy is the ability to create an informative and engaging webpage for your business so that customers can retrieve valuable information concerning your brand, products, and services. Utilizing clear formatting, concise information, and a compelling layout will undoubtedly attract potential customers and enhance your online appeal.

Finally, if you found this book useful in any way, a review on Amazon is always appreciated!

DESCRIPTION

If you are an ambitious business owner with a passion for network marketing and dominating the digital marketplace, then *Network Marketing: The Real Strategy That Converts People into Customers* is the book you have been waiting for!

Each step of the network marketing process requires careful planning and strategic awareness to achieve success. This e-book provides comprehensive methods of developing an effective Facebook Ads campaign as well as creating a formidable YouTube channel. Thereafter, you will learn a step-by-step process of how to merge your YouTube channel with your Facebook page for your business. This will undoubtedly maximize the exposure for your business' marketing content by tapping into the endless users on Facebook.

In an age of an incredible amount of competition from the businesses online, there is limited space in the market. As a result, creating a viable, informative, and compelling webpage for your business is critical. A professional landing page will allow current and potential customers to learn more about your business and, more importantly, buy products right off of your website. While boosting revenue, a viable website will also build trust with customers (current and potential) because of the fact that consumers will trust you with their money through online payments.

With these strategies in mind, reaching your target audience and converting people into customers of your business will be ameliorated immensely. No to mention, this e-book lists and elaborates on the most important questions to ask when developing a webpage for your business so that you leave no stone unturned with regards to your online marketing strategy.

It is time to eliminate harmful and useless strategies from your network marketing approach and delve into the best strategies for the modern digital age. Maximize your business potential with the very best e-book available on the topic of network marketing and gain new customers for your business! So, dive in and buy this business-boosting book today!

Inside you will find:

- How to build a viable online webpage for your business and the best tips for creating a clear user interface.
- The value of refraining from creating closed-group profiles on Facebook for your business strategy.
- Why merging your YouTube channel and Facebook profile will amount to substantial gains in audience exposure and revenue.
- The best tips for successful video presentations and oral communication online.
- How to build a sustainable and loyal audience through a YouTube channel.
- The vast array of changes between the traditional era and the current digital marketing age.

www.ingramcontent.com/pod-product-compliance
Lightning Source LLC
Chambersburg PA
CBHW031556210526
45464CB00003B/1314